The Secret Meaning of Things

Books by Lawrence Ferlinghetti

The Secret Meaning of Things

Lawrence Ferlinghetti

A New Directions Book

Contents

The Secret Meaning of Things

Assassination Raga

Tune in to a raga
on the stereo
and turn on Death TV
without its sound
Outside the plums are growing in a tree
'The force that through the green fuse
drives the flower'
drives Death TV
'A grief ago'
They lower the body soundlessly
into a huge plane in Dallas
into a huge plane in Los Angeles
marked 'United States of America'
and soundlessly
the 'United States of America'

takes off
& wings away with that Body
Tune out the TV sound
& listen soundlessly
to the blind mouths of its motors
& a sitar speaking on the stereo
a raga in a rage
at all that black death
and all that bad karma
La illaha el lill Allah
There is no god but God
The force that through the red fuze
drives the bullet
drives the needle in its dharma groove
and man the needle
drives that plane
of the 'United States of America'
through its sky full of shit & death
and the sky never ends
as it wings soundlessly

from those fucked-up cities
whose names we'd rather not remember
Inside the plane
inside the plane a wife
lies soundlessly
against the coffin
Engine whines as sitar sings outrageously
La illaha el lill Allah
There is no god but God?
There is no god but Death
The plums are falling through the tree
The force that drives the bullet
through the gun
drives everyone
as the 'United States of America'
flies on sightlessly
through the swift fierce years
with the dead weight of its Body
which they keep flying from Dallas
which they keep flying from Los Angeles

And the plane lands
without folding its wings
its shadow in mourning for itself
withdraws into itself
in death's draggy dominion
La illaha el lill Allah
There is no god but Death
The force that through the green fuze
drove his life
drives everyone
La illaha el lill Allah
And they are driving the Body
they are driving the Body
up Fifth Avenue
past a million people in line
'We are going to be here a long time'
says Death TV's spielman
The cortège passes soundlessly
'Goodbye! Goodbye!' some people cry
The traffic flows around & on

The force that drives the cars
combusts our karma
La illaha el lill Allah
There is no god but Death
The force that drives our life to death
drives sitar too
so soundlessly
La illaha el lill Allah
And they lift the Body
They lift the Body
of the United States of America
and carry it into a cathedral
singing Hallelujah He Shall Live
For ever & ever
And then the Body moves again
down Fifth Avenue
Fifty-seven black sedans after it
There are people with roses
behind the barricades
in bargain-basement dresses

And sitar sings & sings nonviolence
sitar sounds in us its images of ecstasy
its depth of ecstasy
against old dung & death
La illaha el lill Allah
La illaha el lill Allah
The force that strikes its strings
strikes us
And the funeral train
the silver train
starts up soundlessly
at a dead speed
over the hot land
an armed helicopter over it
They are clearing the tracks ahead of assassins
The tracks are lined with bare faces
A highschool band in New Brunswick plays
The Battle Hymn of the Republic
They have shot it down again
They have shot him down again

& will shoot him down again

& take him on a train

& lower him again

into a grave in Washington

La illaha el lill Allah

Day & night journeys the coffin

through the dark land

too dark now to see the dark faces

La illaha el lill Allah

Plums & planes are falling through the air

La illaha el lill Allah

as sitar sings the only answer

sitar sings its only answer

sitar sounds the only sound

that still can still all violence

La illaha el lill Allah

There is no god but Life

Sitar says it Sitar sounds it

Sitar sounds on us to love love & hate hate

Sitar breathes its Atman breath in us

sounds & sounds in us its lovely *om om*

La illaha el lill Allah

At every step the pure wind rises

La illaha el lill Allah

People with roses

behind the barricades!

First read, to a loud evening raga, at "The Incredible Poetry Reading," Nourse Auditorium, San Francisco, June 8, 1968, the day Robert Kennedy was buried.

"Death TV": the phrase comes from "So Who Owns Death TV" by William Burroughs, Claude Pélieu & Carl Weissner.

"The force that through the green fuse drives the flower" & "A grief ago": from Dylan Thomas.

"La illaha el lill Allah": variation of a Sufi ecstatic chant. A corruption of the Koran. Sirhan Sirhan also corrupted the Koran.

"the swift fierce years": from a phrase in Eldridge Cleaver's "Soul On Ice."

Atman: breath, soul, life principle.

Om: originally a syllable denoting assent—the "ideal, inaudible sound" of the universe. . . .

Bickford's Buddha

Some days I'm afflicted
with Observation Fever
omnivorous perception of phenomena
not just visual
like today in Bickford's Harvard Square
sitting still seeing everything
watching a lot of beautiful animals
walk by
turning & turning in their courses
A goofy chick at the next table
just escaped a psycho ward
telling everyone she's "a lost squirrel"
and the manager kicking out hippies
and Cambridge Deacon Hell's Angels
I take a trip to the Harvard Co-op
and overhear a bird ask
for "books by Ferlinghetti"
(They dint have none)
The Coop is patrolled by guards
"Uniformed & Ununiformed" the sign says

I read it "Uninformed" first
Came back down the street
digging everything
seeing just how much I could take in
without missing anything
Any thing
Eyeballs faces lips alack
And a threeyearoldgirl on a sidewalk
licking the chocolate spreckles off
a gooey ice-cream cone
peering through the open backdoor
of a drycleaningshop
where some sort of big belted wheel
was going round fast
Missed what kind & went back
& still couldn't tell
Something to do with cleaning things
without wetting them no doubt
a Puritan preoccupation
While I got me own hang-ups
to go round & round with:
really afflicted
with this observation biz
It never stops
on & on & on
"Habitual laissez-faire reaction
to phenomenal stimuli"

Ontological preoccupations
in Plympton Street
in the Grolier Bookshop
Photos of "everybody" on the walls
All the poets that is
who've passed this Blarney Stone
Eliot & Dame Edith
Lowell & Ginsberg & Marianne Moore
Creeley & Duncan & Thom Gunn
Where am I
walking by
not announcing meself
Phooey I'm a poet too?
Still one who walks by
silent
Silence exile & cunning
still after all dese years
even in me own cuntry
& me not even Stephen Daedalus?
But "when guns are roaring
the Muses have no right
to be silent!"
(says a book on Russian poets
I pick up free at Schoenhof's)
Aha/Well/Later
Latah
The angel Deacons are rapping

in front of Bickford's Cafeteria
These are our Revolutionaries?
I'll speak out to them at least
Well/Later/like the politicians say
I got more exploratory studies
to carry out first
before committing myself
I got more observing to do first
I got my affliction to feed
I got my muse to feed
before the guns start roaring
my bird is still hungry
I've not taken in half enough light
phenomenal not noumenal
I've only just begun to fight
A Simmons College coed
who called herself "a rich pushy Jewish chick"
told me the action was here
at Bickford's Cafeteria
better than across the street
in the Harvard Library
where I spend the afternoon
observing readers
observing books
observing others' observations
('Til a guard kicks me out—
no Student Card)

In the Lamont Poetry Room
under the eye of a different drummer
I turn on a voice on a disk
and Othello spins off
and out into the Yard
and across through the gates
to Bickford's
where he accosts a Black Revolutionary
I also observe a pale lecturer
with a neck-mike in class
addressing himself to
"Neo-Freudians & Anti-Freudians"
He has very small pudgy hands
and rimless eyeglasses
he doesn't know are Camp
I contemplate his being
neither Anti nor Neo
By four in the afternoon
they've brushed off the angels at Bickford's
They fly away
Back in a quad a spring bird sings
through a Linden tree
which has just succeeded
in making its buds into leaves
A squirrel is lost among them
Someone is taking pictures
in front of a statue of—

Whodunit?
A screw-faced Jewish kid sits down
on the stone base of the statue
His fat mother sits down too
with her black handbag
and strange shoes
He is turning his Screw
A bird continues
A cricket
winds his watch
The father says "stand up"
and he takes their picture
for eternity
(Photo of "Allen Ginsberg & Mother
NY World's Fair 1939"
flashes in memory's movie)
What could that mean
And what could be
the secret meaning of this day
& of what's been so blindly observed?
There's no such thing as an accident
the post-Freudians say
The statue says
                    John Harvard
                    Founder
                    1638
He is sitting in a heavy bronze chair

meant to be wood
He wears buckle shoes
like John Lennon
and has long long hands
on a big open bronze book
meant to be paper
& eternal
The bird continues
I now note two bronze books
under John's chair
He has long hippie hair
and a dreamy look
his eyes on the grass
not the book
Probably really a non-student
no Student Card
A bearded student buddha
in blue-jeans beads & sneakers
treads by heavily
snorting into a harmonica
his American mantra
The bird continues
its dharani
I continue on
to the Fogg Museum
and see askant the sexy Bodhisattva Maitreya
standing in the gold bronze light

of Nepal
and the wood Bodhisattva Kuan Yin
seated in "the position of royal ease"
looks through me seeing everything
or Nothing
as I split for Kirkland House
late now for my poetry reading
hurrying along seeing all too clearly
another thousand things anew
to scribe
No time now
for the Position of Royal Ease
No time now to "leave behind
all phenomenal distinction"
and so become all-seeing Buddha
A baby motors by in an electric stroller
An Angel revs his hog
Life roars past too fast
I see askant all too clearly
how all is imaginary & all passes
Yet how can the imaginary pass?
At Kirkland Hotel so-called
the biddy-in-charge
takes me for a young stud
informing me gratuitously
I can't have "visitors" in my room
I see all too clearly how

he who travels alone
arrives alone
No place here
for the Position of Royal Ease
Time in some later reincarnation
to lie down in silence
without cunning
I see all too clearly how
poor dear flesh fumbles on
into eternity
as I rush on
to my Boston poetry reading
The sun slips down
into Boston proper
A bird continues
A bard hangs out his tongue
What right has bird or buddha
to be silent
in the Dublin of America?

Writ on the back of a map of Harvard College

All Too Clearly

A touch of old surrealism today
at a stoplight in La Jolla
Lotte Lehmann
on the car radio
singing in German 1919
sounding like an old newsreel
of a drowning Valkyrie
A Blue Rider appears & the light changes
to tomorrow on the blue grass
of Reinhard Lettau's backyard
listening to Marlene Dietrich moan
"Jonny" she sings in smoky German
"Jonny when your birthday comes
I'll be your guest all night
Jonny I love you so much
If you only had a birthday every day
How about coming some afternoon
at half past four?"
During the song I go to the phone
and call my half sister

We have never been very close
yet we have
I make a date for lunch
and the song ends
in a Berlin cellar
Reinhard in his Jean-Paul Sartre glasses
and Véronique his Berlin chick
with the deep black eye-circles
and a Mao Tse Tung button
go with me for lunch
to a straight seafood place
near the airport
My sister orders Blue Fish
and after some debate
we get Marine Bowls looking like
frozen dead aquariums
of shrimp squid scallops
stuck in mayonnaise they
          can't swim thru
We succeed in eating them
          with conversations about
          frozen Siberia
          Check Point Charley
          and the Berlin Hilton
My sister's mother
          also comes up
          distantly

like a beautiful white iceberg
seen off the port bow
closer than one had expected
yet still unapproachable
We skirt the subject carefully
knowing that most of the story
          is underwater
yet uncertain where it ends
(She is in fact at this moment
approaching us on a South Seas cruise ship
soon to dock)
We end up at the airport
where I emplane alone
In the upper air there are no white icebergs
and also no Blue Angels
What is this place
where no sea maid's song
may reach us
and what is the secret meaning
of this poem adrift in air
Every day the news gets more surreal
Dark crowds still flow over London Bridge
even as it is transported
stone by stone
to Arizona
And every day
a line of love's battleships is sunk

by invisible fish
And there are days
when I see all too clearly
And there are days
when I am everyone I meet
A cold goddess in miniskirt
collects my ticket
& adjusts my seat

1 Mar 68

Through the Looking Glass

I. Imagining LSD

Deep blue haze
                    Elektra wings thru
        Illimitable
White bird in it
                far off
                    skimming
    or a white plane skating
                    way down there
        small shadow of it
                    sweeping
                        the shrunk landscape
                disappeared now
                        into the great brown ground

as if fallen
while its plane still flies on
miraculously!
And Sunday Chicago appears
at end of Autumn carpet
stuck to great flat blue cloud
of Lake Michigan
stretched out
Rich resorts & Lakeshore fronts
beaches lapped forever
pavilions asleep in time
Hum of Elektra winging down
wigging down
Seatbelts on
flaps down
swinging around
for re-entry
into that world
Engine drones
like a tamboura

Passage to India

               on LSD Airlines

     Temporary flight

                  of ecstatic insanity

        into its own

                glittering terminals

                    pulsing with light

Gliding down & down

How calm all

Still autumn forest

            Golf-link in it

Straightwayhighway into a cloverleaf

               cars crawling the petals

Huge cemetery in brown woods

           Death itself only another

              lower form

          of temporary ecstatic insanity

         out of your skull

                into the ground

How soft the trees down there
                    How very soft
                              from up here
          We
                    could almost
                    bounce into them
          soft landing
                    among the branches
And so on down
                    into it
                    into the soft ground
                    illusion!
          As if
                    as if we don't ever die
                    but become new burrowing consciousnesses
                              Earthworm Tractors
ZOOM
          Still a scary landing
                    into *that* Underground

II. LSD, Big Sur

Great progress!

        thru the looking glass with 'Alice'

Ten years of dreams

        in the green forest

Uplands

        of the imagination

        Far green grottoes

Future books

        of the Illuminati

        writ out there

        across the landscape—

        land escape—

        into ecstasy

Intolerable arabesques
            coming & coming & coming
                on & on
                        toward me
                    onto me
                        over me
        Relentless
            Ineffable!
                Coming down now
                        re-echoing
                    gliding down
                            those landscapes
                & arabesques of earth
                seas reglitterized
        seen thru a silkscreen overlay
                    sun stricken!
On & on & on
        it still keeps coming
                out there/up there
        keeps going on & on

over the horizon

into eternity

now that the cries of the birds

has stopped

O I alone

walk the red heavens

the first blind steps

in the direction

of some dharma

whose name I could

conceivably sing

yet cannot yet decipher

III. After-dream

The soft fur parted
but he withdrew
from around her body
his halcyon limbs
and allowed the Ram
only Shiva and Contemplation

And Shiva advanced
with a broken arm

After the Cries of the Birds

Hurrying thru eternity
    after the cries of the birds has stopped
I see the "future of the world"
     in a new visionary society
    now only dimly recognizable
    in folk-rock ballrooms
     free-form dancers in ecstatic clothing
     their hearts their gurus
      every man his own myth
      butterflies in amber
        caught fucking life
 hurrying thru eternity
     to a new pastoral era
I see the shadows of that future
   in that white island
      which is San Francisco
   floating in its foreign sea
       seen high on a hill
     in the Berkeley Rose Garden
   looking West at sunset to the Golden Gate

adrift in its Japanese landscape
under Mt. Tamal-Fuji
with its grazing bulls
hurrying thru heaven
the city with its white buildings
"a temple to some unknown god"
(as Voznesensky said)
after the cries of the birds has stopped
I see the sea come in
over South San Francisco
and the island of the city
truly floated free at last
never really a part of America
East East and West West
and the twain met long ago
in "the wish to pursue what lies beyond
the mind"
and with no place to go but In
after Columbus recovered America
and the West Coast captured by some
Spanish Catholics
cagily getting the jump by sea
coveredwagons crawling over lost plains
hung up in Oklahoma
Prairie schooners into Pullmans
while whole tribes of Indians
shake hopeless feather lances

and disappear over the horizon
to reappear centuries later
feet up and smoking wild cigars
at the corner of Hollywood & Vine
hurrying thru eternity
must we wait for the cries of the birds
to be stopped
before we dig In
after centuries of running
up & down the Coast of West
looking for the right place to jump off
further Westward
the Gutenberg Galaxy casts its light no further
the "Westward march of civilization"
comes to a dead stop on the shores of
Big Sur Portland & Santa Monica
and turns upon itself at last
after the cries of the birds has stopped
must we wait for that
to dig a new model
of the universe
with instant communication
a world village
in which every human being is a part of us
though we be still throw-aways
in an evolutionary progression

as Spengler reverses himself
          Mark Twain meets Jack London
          and turns back to Mississippi
          shaking his head
     and the Last Frontier
                    having no place to go but In
     can't face it
               and buries its head
Western civilization gone too far West
                    might suffer a sea-change
          into Something Else Eastern
                         and that won't do
     The Chinese are coming anyway
                    time we prepared their tea
     Gunga Din still with us
          Kipling nods & cries *I told you so!*
          the French King hollers *Merde!*
               and abandons his Vietnam bordel
but not us
               we love them too much for that
     though the Mayflower turned around sets sail again
     back to Plymouth England (and the
                              Piltdown letdown)
     misjudging the coast & landing in Loverpool
     American poets capture Royal Albert Hall
          The Jefferson Airplane takes off
                         and circles heaven

It all figures
                    in a new litany
                                        probably pastoral
after the cries of the birds has stopped
          Rose petals fall
                         in the Berkeley Rose Garden
where I sit trying to remember
                    the lines about rose leaves
 in the *Four Quartets*
                    S*ella kisses her lover in the sunset
                              under an arbor
          A Los Angeles actor nearby goes *Zap! Zap!*
                    at the setting sun
It is the end
               I drop downhill
          into a reception for Anaïs Nin
               with a paperbag full of rose leaves
She is autographing her Book
          I empty the bag over her head from behind
          Her gold lacquered hair sheds the petals
               They tumble red & yellow on her
                                        signed book
          Girl again she presses them
                         between the leaves
                    delightedly
                              like fallen friends
               Her words

flame in my heart
Virginia Woolf under water
she drifts away on the book
a leaf herself blowing skittered
over the horizon
The wish to pursue what lies beyond the mind
lies just beyond
Ask a flower what it does
to move beyond the senses
Our cells hate metal
The tide turns
We shoot holes in the clouds' trousers
and napalm sears the hillsides
skips a bridge
narrows to a grass hut full of charred bodies
and is later reported looking like
"The eternal flame at Kennedy's grave"
A tree flowers red It can't run

Shall we now advance into the 21st century?
I see the lyric future of the world
on the beaches of Big Sur
gurus at Jack's Flats
nude swart maidens swimming
in pools of sunlight

Kali on the beach
guitarists with one earring
lovely birds in long dresses and Indian headbands

What does this have to do with Lenin?
Plenty!
Die-hard Maoists lie down together crosswise
and out comes a string
of Chinese firecrackers
and after the cries of the birds
has stopped
Chinese junks show up suddenly
off the coast of Big Sur
filled with more than Chinese philosophers
dreaming they are butterflies
How shall we greet them? Are we ready
to receive them?
Shall we put out koan steppingstones
scrolls & bowls
greet them with *agape*
Tu Fu and bamboo flutes at midnight?
Big Sur junk meet
Chinese junk?
Will they ride the breakers into Bixby Cove?
Will they bring their women with them
Will we take them on the beach
like Ron Boise's lovers in Kama Sutra

face them with Zen zazen & tea
made from the dust of the wings
of butterflies dreaming
they're philosophers?
Or meet them with last war's tanks
roaring out of Fort Ord
down the highways & canyons
shooting as they come
flame-throwers flaming jelly
into the Chinese rushes
under the bridge at Bixby?
The U.S. owns the highway but is Big Sur
in the USA?
San Francisco floats away
beyond the three-mile limit
of the District of Eternal Revenue
No need to pay your taxes
The seas come in to cover us
Agape we are & agape we'll be

*First read at the Literarisches Colloquium in Berlin, 1967,
on a program with Andrei Voznesensky.*

Moscow in the Wilderness, Segovia in the Snow

Midnight Moscow Airport
      sucks me in from Siberia
And blows me out alone
          in a black bus
        down dark straight night roads
        stark snow plains
        eternal taiga
          into monster Moscow
     stands of white birches
        ghosted in the gloaming
Where of a sudden
      Segovia bursts thru
         over the airwaves
They've let him in
         to drive the dark bus
Segovia's hands
        grasp the steering wheel
Yokels in housing projects
    drop their balalaikas & birch banjos

Segovia comes on
        like the pulse of life itself
Segovia comes on thru the snowdrifts
            and plains of La Mancha
        fields & fields & fields
            of frozen music
        melted on bus radios
Segovia at the instrument
            driving thru the night land
    of Antiquera
            Granada
                Seville
        Tracery of the Alhambra
        in a billion white birches
            born in the snow
        trills of blackbirds in them
Segovia warms his hands
            and melts Moscow
        moves his hand
            with a circular motion
            over an ivory bridge
            to gutted Stalingrads
Segovia knows no answer
He's no Goya & he's no Picasso
but also
        he's no Sleeping Gypsy With Guitar
        Guarded by a Lion

and who knows if he slept
                                with Franco
He knows black condors fly
He knows a free world when he hears one
His strums are runs upon it
He does not fret
He plucks his guts
and listens to himself as he plays
and speaks to himself
and echoes himself
And he keeps driving & driving
                                his instrument
        down the wide dark ways
                        into great Moscow
        down the black boulevards
                past Kremlin lit & locked
                        in its hard dream
                in the great Russian night
        past Bolshoi Ballet & Gorky Institute
                John Reed at the Drama Theatre
                        Stalyagi & heroin at Taganka
Stone Mayakovsky stares
                thru a blizzard of white notes
                        in Russian winter light
Segovia hears his stoned cry
        and he hears the pulse in the blood

as he listens to life as he plays
and he keeps coming & coming
              thru the Russian winter night
He's in Moscow but doesn't know it
He played somewhere else
              and it comes out here
in a thaw on an airwave
              over Gogol's Dark People
  stark figures
              in the white night streets
  clotted in the snow
He listens to them as he goes along
He listens for a free song
              such as he hardly hears
              back home
              Is Lenin listening
              after fifty Octobers
Segovia walks thru the snow
              listening as he goes
    down Vorovsky Street
              to the Writers' Union
He meets the old hairs that run it
  They dig him
              & they know what it means to dig
              in mahogany cities
Segovia teaches them open-tuning

with which they can play anything
  freely & simply
 This is not his Master Class
He leaves them humming & goes on
Segovia plays in the loose snow
  and digs a bit alone
   under the free surface
    with his free hand
He strikes softly as he listens
He hears a dull thud
  where something is buried
   a familiar thud
  such as he sometimes hears
   back home
He turns away & goes on
    down Vorovsky Street
His music has a longing sound
He yearns & yet docs not yearn
He exists & is tranquil
   in spite of all
He has no message
He is his own message
  his own ideal sound
And he sounds so lonely to himself
  as he goes on playing
   in the iron-white streets

And he is saying: I say all I know
       & I know no meaning
He is saying
       This is the song of evening
       when the sphinx lies down
       This is the song of the day
       that begins & begins
       The night lifts
              its white night-stick
       The ash of life
              dries my song
       If you only knew
He is saying
       My love my love
              where are you
       Under the pomegranate tree
He is saying
       Where is joy where is ecstasy
       stretched out in the snow
       where only the birds are at home
He is saying
       There's a huge emptiness here
       that stares from all the faces
       All that is lost must be
              looked for once more
He is saying

Far from me far from me
you are the hour & the generation
they marked for result
He is saying
I am your ruin
unique & immortal
I am your happiness unknown
I am light
where you are dark
where you are heavy
He is saying
I am an old man
and life flowers
in the windows of the sun
But where is the sun the sun
Soleares . . .
On the steps of a jail
that looks like a church
he finds a white bird
What is important in life? says the bird
Segovia says Nada but keeps on playing
his Answer
And he cries out now
when he sees a strange woman

                or sees a strange thing
       And he hears many strange women
            & many strange things
            after fifty Octobers
            & fifty strange springs
And Segovia follows them
            down their streets
            and into their houses
            and into their rooms
            and into the night of their beds
       And waits for them to make love
       And waits for them to speak
       And waits & waits for them to speak
And he cries out now
       when he hears them speak
            at last in their last retreat
No he doesn't cry out
He never cries out
He is taciturn & never sings
Only his instrument speaks & sings
But when it does sing
when it does cry out
at what it hears
                an ancient armadillo
            asleep for centuries
                in the cellar of the Kremlin

raises its horny head
        opens its square third eye
and looks around blinking
    and then at last
    unglues its great gut mouth
        and utters
                ecstatic static

Moscow-San Francisco
March, 1967

Dedicated to my friends
Andrei Voznesensky
     &
Yevgeni Yevtushenko

New Directions Paperbooks—A Partial Listing

For complete listing request free catalog from
New Directions, 80 Eighth Avenue, New York 10011   †Bilingual

For complete listing request free catalog from
New Directions, 80 Eighth Avenue, New York 10011

†Bilingual